Everything in the Universe

Everything in the Universe

poems

Amy Wright

Iris Press
Oak Ridge, Tennessee

COVER ARTWORK: *Future Primeval*
Copyright © 2008 by Suzanne Stryk
mixed media

BOOK DESIGN: Robert B. Cumming, Jr.

Library of Congress Cataloging-in-Publication Data

Names: Wright, Amy, 1975- author.
Title: Everything in the universe : poems / Amy Wright.
Description: Oak Ridge, Tennessee : Iris Press, [2016]
Identifiers: LCCN 2016010303 | ISBN 9781604542370 (pbk. : alk. paper)
Classification: LCC PS3623.R5 A6 2016 | DDC 811/.6—dc23
LC record available at http://lccn.loc.gov/2016010303

Acknowledgments

With thanks to the editors of these journals for publishing the following poems in earlier versions.

Baltimore Review: "Scientists Film Inside A Flying Insect"
Birmingham Poetry Review: "Red-eyed Treehopper" (as *Platycotis*), Bird-dung Mimic" (as *Notocera*)
Blast Furnace: "Scarab"
Bodega: "Sharpshooters" (as *Graphocephala*)
Calyx: "Specimens, Mount 4," "Specimens, Mount 28"
Canary: "Lepidoptery"
Cimarron Review: "*Still Life with Flowers, Shells, and Insects*"
The Collagist: "Bioluminescence"
DMQ Review: "Old Glassy Speaks Her Peace"
Green Briar Review: "Of Course"
Hollins Critic: "Girlhood's Navy"
Kenyon Review: "*Micrographia, or, Some Physiological Observations of Minute Bodies Made by Magnifying Glasses with Observations and Inquiries thereupon*"
Ohio Edit: "Biophilia," "Insect Time," "Living like Earwigs" (as *Forficula*)
POOL Poetry: "Flower Beetle" (as *Agestrata*), "Citrus Longhorn" (as *Anoplophora*), "Yam Weevil" (as *Eupholus*), "Titanic" (as *Titanus*), "Featherwings" (as *Nanosella*)
Prick of the Spindle: "Ten Thousand Car Hood Lakes Shimmering After Rain," "A Bloody-nosed Beetle…," "Long-tongued Flower Sipper"
Round Table: "Getting the Bird Out"
Salamander: "Collage of Thirty Dragonfly Species Headshots"
The Southern Poetry Anthology, Volume VI: "Tornado Warning"
The Account: A Journal of Poetry, Prose, and Thought: "Hymenopus"
The Labletter: "*Cimex Cerebrum*," "Of the Feet of Flies"
Your Impossible Voice: "Acres Green©"
The Volta: "Inside Every Fried Pie"

I would also like to thank my mother, Dan Corrie, Todd Dills, Kaaren Engel, Susannah Felts, Eileen G'Sell, April Ossmann, and Adam Vines for their feedback and encouragement on these poems.

Contents

III.

IV.

For Don

Inside every Fried Pie

Considering that every fifth living thing is a beetle, insect poetics might be said to be about scale. Or span—since midges, mayflies, and mosquitos have colonized air, land, and sea from the Sahara to Antarctica. Or, since for every human being Earth hosts about 300 pounds of insects, heft.

Or time—as kin to silverfish circling our bathtub drains traversed dinosaur dung, their ancestors emerging 420 million years before Baal-worshipers.

As if the top of my head were being nibbled, I ponder their family's individualism.

The lens that could encompass such magnitude justified monotheism. Then cracked. Linnaeus died an unhappy man, his life's work of taking species two by two names into the catalog endless as Sisyphus's.

And what of the intergalactic translation, considering the distance from sonogram to alphabet? Do the cadences treehoppers thrum across neem branches not mean but be, their concert forever irreducible? And doesn't such a radically different system of communication alter beauty's definition.

An aesthetic trussed to usefulness, the orb weaver's form follows more than function. Biology's brass knuckles glitter with a comely luster. As if reason tatted this planet's garments, lifted in celebration of all that checkers infinity's niches. I might even call it Appalachian, bound as it keeps being to salvage something from nothing, and that something sumptuous as a butter-full cauldron of mason bee-pollinated apples.

I.

Biodiversity is all we have.

—E.O. Wilson

Flower Beetle

Agestrata, your
exoskeleton's polished
metal acid trip mirror
reflects bug-eyed cousins
whose profit margins differ
markedly from your
glam getup's luminous
beauty, 70's disco gypsy
otherworld holdover
come to show earthlings
how to shimmer, and shake
our pygidia, grove on
multiplicity's iris-
dilating orchestra.

Lepidoptery

Grandfather, auto mechanic, lepidopterist
in the posture of upright fence, Tom
peers into oak groves.

Plain-clothed, no blaze-orange earflaps
outfit him for the annual buck
moth emergence,

in hunting season, though he bears a long-handled
net and local farmer's permission
in lieu of a rifle or license.

After working all his life with his hands,
he knows where to hold the thorax
to relax these downy winders, keep their crushed

velvet scales perfect as a layer of baklava.
His blue Ford parked by the roadside,
what he wants before retirement

is to breed a female. He anticipates
with a fisherman's patience, sights the distance
for a falling leaf to animate, beeline

behind him where a gravy-tailed egg-layer
calls, knows a flake of planet dander
will break free from the hard

wood, fly toward him, an Isadora
Duncan comet on the horizon will careen
into his steady-widening orbit,

him waiting
with a forked twig in a fastfood bag,
his little golden years luxury.

Micrographia, or, Some Physiological Observations
of Minute Bodies Made by Magnifying Glasses
with Observations and Inquiries thereupon

Without Robert Hooke,
curious Charles II
might glimpse a flea
hop on a dog's
back to suck a drop,
or the paw scratch his
own hide off to find
the flick, but only
under magnification
might a scientist
witness the beast's *suit*
of sable Armour
shield that gambit
as it tucks foreleg A
(drawn and explained
to his Highness)
into B, and C
into D, later named
tibia, femur, trochanter,
coxa by those who would
jettison now common
knowledge to train
their sights on other
planets, while the flea
keeps stacking its springs
to launch unforeseeable
distances entrusted
to a similar idea
of progress.

Red-eyed Treehopper

Like an out-of-towner
blazing through downtown
Chester County in a Lamborghini,
only the size of a southern
belle's broken pink fingernail—
you look a bit wild
for a mother, standing sentinel
over nymphs with brazen
yellow wing markings,
but whose to judge a turkey
oak dweller from Florida
who repulses vespid wasps
who threaten her colony,
befriends ants with honeydew
the way fifties wives used to
woo new neighbors?
If mother's little helper suckles
sap while males prolong sex
twenty-four hours if possible,
scientists deem the tradeoff
mutual, since the last to mate
is borne into the future via
forty eggs like corpses escorted
from the nest by a six-legged
housecleaning army.

Citrus Longhorn

To the single
adult *Anoplophora*
intercepted at an Athens,
Georgia nursery on a crape
myrtle bonsai shipment
from China, I say no
attempts are being made
to Cadillac-grill mount
your headgear décor,
twilit fruit pest, your dorsum
a painter's drop cloth
daubed with white speckles
prompting the moniker
starry sky, sky beetle
from someone who saw you
simply, pretty quarantine,
gave you a beautiful name
like Anaktoria as anodyne
for hatred you rebuff,
being so loved by night
you wear its beaming
senseless as plum fruit
under wax bloom.

Still Life with Flowers, Shells, and Insects

(1635) Balthasar Van der Ast

After apprenticeship
to flower painter
Bosschaert the Elder,
Balthasar branched out,
posed conch shells
beside emperor tulip
and earwig, elicited
pears' kinetic nature
with crustaceans,
exhibited the paradox
of still life with a viewer-
perusing petal-fresh
caterpillar, oblivious
as the greenest virgin
outstretched to sniff
air for decay.

Bird-dung Mimic

A tenderfoot tribe's
adaptation to predation
eludes most Internet notice
with its piebald body
camouflage. Creatures make
more kinds of living than we
imagine, surfing gossip
columns for the options fame
or money opens. Fortune
may elevate the homeliest
to matrimony or sequester
choice lulus in neotropical
regions. *Notocera*'s symphony
stayed private until sonograms
recorded courtship coos
tapped on plant stems' substrata
now aired on wireless networks
that chat about data breaches
but offer no semantic theory
when two headphoned biologists
touch ginger fingers to ears,
eyes floating left, assent
drum licks throbbing tree limbs
farther in than wind, grin
hoping to finesse their coupling.

Collage of Thirty Dragonfly Species Headshots

Note the pseudopupils—from a pencil eraser
fleck to an ant's foreleg, pinpricks in the blue
foveal band indiscernible to untrained eyes,
nuclei-less whorl of dollhouse door locust grain

where a petaltail scouts a swallowtail.
One might stumble hours inside closed buildings,
fall heat-of-the-day tired onto a lawn rattling with cicadas
where students glean meter and vie

for notice, reading Emily Dickinson, oblivious
to poetic distinctions between such moonstone lenses,
heavy-lidded opals, vitreous kyanites—
beauty rare as larimars, inside which trillions

of genetic modifications uplift clypei, incline
prothoraxes by micrometers slight as pupils
sliding toward beloved crushes, or one engagement
ring rising higher than another's fingered angle.

These all eyes are cool, scanned
before they lose refrigeration's stupor,
fly into the bright background where one Susan
shines extra ultraviolet among a field of black-eyed strangers.

Specimens, Mount 4

Stag Beetle

Pierced with a gold pin,
you copper-antlered trophy
are almost a buck, but
miniatures menace
only minor catastrophes

Disarticulated Beetle

Antenna, thorax, maxilla,
genitalia—even your hind wing
membrane spread like sheets,
immodestly

Lampyridae

Firefly fossil
entombed in sap stone, light
gobbled by a centuries-old setting
of trapped-air pearls

Ant Lion

Pitfall makers
surprise slippers
into sand funnels
and paradigm planners
when you fledge lace wings

Featherwings

Beetles small
enough to enter a fungus spore
are hidden among us
without lenses,
depicted in drawings
to comfort introvert
experts on websites.

Moon-headed True Bug

Hydra antennae's planetary
appendages moved Arthur Heller
to sculpt plasticine and galalith
replicas worth one year of
dexterous opposable-thumb-wielding
labor. Seven hundred thirty eight bristles
grace the Natural History Museum's
thorn-crowned *Globulare*, though any old
globe-bearing treehopper might lay another
dozen prototypes en masse in glory
bush tissue, assuming saucer-eyed
onlookers can keep said leaves available.

Unflappable Cohabitants

Aussie naturalists, Wade and
Lisa spotted an as yet unnamed
Anubis in a parking-lot-
adjacent eucalyptus. Drawn
too to the 12-kilo woodland
refugium that fostered these
millipedes rent from kin
in undeveloped outskirts,
they unsuspected
jackal-like genitalia
unlike any other species
on this endemic island
where interlopers booted
so many others out.
Park visitors, rather than
specialists, they noticed only
that standout yellow
against white bark.

Dragonfly Sutra

Zuni depictions
of twice-swiped crosses

single out less than most people
ubiquitous dragonfly species

from endangered Hine's Emeralds
who inhabit the same muck

fens and calcareous
marshes. Manitoba prairie-grass

catches can't happen unless
spinylegs deploy

landing gear, and needling
north to Ontario is a no-go

without aerodynamic
shoulder patches,

but, like axle-stripped
Thunderbirds, minimalist drawings

suggest how one part
can down the whole

plant on which
cities depended.

Bioluminescence

To enjoy something,
like *jiu-jitsu* or *capoeira*,
is to stumble onto a sensation
that stops you, gets you looking
for newer models of introduction.
Confused, we wonder, should we
bow before or after, kiss *l'éstranger*,
and which cheek, right or left?
If only we lit up, illuminants
pre-equipped to tiki torch ourselves,
we might be fearless, peel back
any darkness for a nice *chénpí*
without hesitation—except
even those beetles with internal
lights run opposite of autonomous
when their pulsing synchronizes,
frightening the young ones
with glimpses of the whole
forest, themselves scattered
at large within it.

Tornado Warning

A siren insists brusquely for us to "take shelter
immediately," at which point, cluster flies
flutter to a windowless first floor copy room
where we sip coffee and joke about bomb shelters,
food rations, and someone muses what it would be like,
to—you know—safely, watch a funnel
touch down, which is happening
in the air vent and the next town over,
though no one's going to chase it.
Doubtless this conversation mirrors a thousand
similarly wasted moments in which no one confesses
how much they hunger and hurt daily, as if a great wind
has already sucked them up from the center, whirled
them into an infinite vacuum of aloneness,
if they can bear to be so very much together
& separate.

II.

When we try to pick out anything by itself, we find it hitched to everything else in the Universe.

—John Muir

Everything in the Universe

The scorpionfly's innocuous wagger
recalls the grounded version's
caudal stinger, though harmless

presenting saliva truffles
to potential partners,
become assassins

if the transaction smacks unsound.
Conjure lemons, *Panorpa communis,*
download a Country Time ad,

since you're hitched to us too.
Every quantum right
or wrong gone liaison

connecting us like body spray-
pervaded locker rooms
or carbon emissions.

Anthrax-laced envelopes
bias senate interns
against indigenous Alaskans'

musk-ox-fur offerings, but Cipro
pharmaceutical stocks rise
as expected.

Nevadan nuclear-plant monkeys
wrench North Korea,
and vice versa. Boat strikes

strand sperm whales in Pacifica.
Buggy software links remotest Africa
to London faster than Sooty Shearwaters

migrate from Falkland Islands
to the Arctic,
or an Arkansas auctioneer

closes bids on an Amish piesafe,
but
neonicitoided sunflowers

down honeybees faster
than Jason Sutfin's pet rosy boa
sends cheerleader skirts flying.

Water bears dryer than attic spiders
animate after rainfall-less decades,
mass-extinction survivors

that comfort climatologists
alone in labs crunching numbers
while Zeus

photobombs the most recent
mortal he's entered
via satellite selfie.

Velvet Ant

Your red coat alerts us
not to touch, but what
felt-pelted bristles glisten
in aposematic signal
to stay back. Ant you are
not, wasp, nor can your
wingless females kill cows,
if your sting is enough
to make manhandlers
wish themselves dead.
Hightailing it down
the walk, that velour duff
a synapse sounding
the collective organ
we mistake constantly
as unconscious.

Biomimicry

There are those who
model rainwater-collecting
garages on termite fortresses,
tincture roots sick chimps seek,
emulate dandelion-planting
bobwhites. No jay scattershot
the Army's John Hancock,
burying loblollies
equidistant as infantrymen
on African-American
gentry's tobacco fields
under eminent domain,
after all. But nature's prototypes
too are stingy as woodstars,
inexplicable as aphids
galling succulent new growth,
illustrative as some seven billion
watery bodies of deciding
continental divides.

Thermoregulation

Highway workers
bow into dog-day-heat-
licked armpits,

brow swipe.
A Confederate flag
at their backs

fans the overpass,
enflames drivers
from New York

to Florida, smoldering
oil-thick rivers
of gasoline-fume-like

fury cracked
windows air.
To vent

the same midday
sunbeat, dragonflies
top switchgrass,

tilt end up, pennants
at full mast
that, in contrast,

grow cool
as Rebel dead,
lower themselves.

Cytoskeleton

I.

The whip-smart, 24/7 embedded
trainer. The stable

plait mother pursed
with folded tissues.

Macrocosm's backup. A walnut
shell's oiled banister.

Fly-tape-adhesive the basement
membrane. The bounded

galaxy, a sponge-cake-fed buttress.
Every muscle contraction a keratin murmuration!

Sirius's helical path mapped
in starfish and lone star ticks.

II.

A protein mosaic [Peters]. A scaffold to organize the contents of the
cell in space [Fletcher].

Every nod couched in 25-nanometer-cylinder synchrony
[Herrmann].

Hollow lattice. From the Greek *kytos*, used in Aristophanes' sense
to mean the cell of a hive of wasps or bees; divided whole.

Living like Earwigs

Exemplary mothers, earwigs linger
after delivery, turn their brood's eggs over easy,

guard them until maturity.
Finding their clutch disturbed,

they undertake midday moves,
vanquish cold-blooded stereotypes.

But given the breast, we demand more,
commend mum only after she sews

strawberry sundresses with matching purses
like Christa Lewis' mother, hand-scoops

487 melon-ball wedding appetizers,
bequeaths chestnut wardrobes early,

while earwig young proliferate continents
where care is not quantifiable—

the countless ones she keeps anyway
from eating one another.

Dragonhunter

A Dragonhunter sails into the backseat
on a Shenandoah Valley breeze.

Six-inch wingspan outlined in black
like hairpin lace panties. The largest clubtail

in North America, a.k.a. Adder Bolt,
Fleeing Snake, *Giuda* (Judas in Italian)

whose sex is roughest of all dragonfly species
for the females.

With punctured eye sockets, disheveled dames
fly to water, lay eggs on leaf litter,

leave nymphs for years in polluted rivers.
This planet may yet return to sharks' and crinoids'

salad days, feather stars littering the sea floor,
Africa colliding with North America,

fulgurant-lensed mourners battling headwinds
to pay respects to each good-looking corpse.

Cobra Lily

No quick death
do you grant ants
who pitch unsuspecting
down your hairy gullet,
Darlingtonia. Your mincemeat-
making juices unpalatable
as Eden's apples. At least,
perhaps that stained
glass-like leaf light
gilds permanent guests'
resting place, if its
sweet scent deceives us,
spawns sinister-cathedral
apostates attended by
decomp deacons,
your pastor, John Torrey,
the ducky omnivore
who named you
after another botanist.

Snipe

All my life, I've been conditioned
not to attempt the risible hunt.
"Catch us one or two," men smirk
of naïfs lured to woods and left
to fail that gullibility test
everyone is in on—save this Midas-
stroked fly on the chair, wings a smoky
web, two wide eyes
on either side of its velvet head.

Titanic

At six and a half inches,
Titanus giganteus outmatches a wallet
the shade of its burnished brown,
shoe-leather-tough skeleton.
Though hundreds of conspicuous
specimens have been pinned in
Colombia, not one larva
has been witnessed downing
the grubs we know they must
in decaying rain forest matter
—and since they stop feeding
by adulthood, we can only
imagine those voracious jaws
working to acquire a life
time of nutrients, strength
enough to snap
pencils if cornered
in temperatures inadequate
to lift an armored chopper
above plethora of no exits.

Dickinson's Bees

Happy

Whistle once and bumbles
flee the dark belt
of a note. Zest is kin to this
rot hen-of-the-woods
mushrooms fruit. A lark
is not bee but part
of the park bees keep up.

Joyful

One never grows allergic
to shy, wooded-avenue
figures inclined to vanish
when presence becomes overbearing
as mastiffs bounding leashless to scatter leaf piles.
Who wouldn't want to be swept,
honey-fueled, over singed earth
blown cool with impending
winter breezes, your dearest knitting
golden groceries around you.

Sublime

A dianthus may disappoint
after April's Dame Rocket stopovers,
yet the queen knows a sensation
drones miss. Between each hill
of breath lie clearings they never notice
in flight, where nothing vies for more
attention than her increased self.

Excited

Hives begin as cavity,
a trunk coated with propolis,
then a queen sniffed.
After which eggs never stop
bobbing forth, gumballs at a factory
of chewing workers wadding saliva-sticky pieces,
pollen beading against clover-fueled chests—
throbbing engines whose tanks
will never run out.

The World's Unkissed Custodian

Blue-black beetles whip meringue loam
only to join it, become ferns
that curl like a struck child
when poked.

Three-year-old Paige unearths
the Earth in miniature,
a pill bug between finger and thumb
like a distant moon.

Cooing,
she pets it, trowel dropped, all digging checked
to coax its clench loose,
woo this hidden life out.

Scarab

Another dead man's
heart swapped

for another living
scarab, sprung Athena-like

from dung.
Sun-roller, emerald

rival hung alive
on horse tack, dangled

from ball gowns, thousands
of luminous beetles

mashed
to find their chemical trigger

matches our muscles
during contraction,

only cold light
loses no heat.

Beneath the sheets,
a chest floods

even the open window
with something like blood.

III.

He put fell poison in the serpent's fang,
Bade wolves to prowl and made the sea to swell,
Shook down honey from the leaves, hid fire away...
then Mariners grouped the stars and gave them names

—Virgil

Biophilia

After E.O. Wilson, who coined the theory

We distrust forces we can't divorce,
but gravity doesn't zigzag
one to light by a true lover's knot,
or tidal eddies trip his retreat;
the gauge that draws air
from the chest when,
curious or kin, he circles back
hasn't been invented yet.

Girlhood's Navy

Katydid cymbals crash open windows,
       forewing-rowed ships crest
            hemlocks, a famously dark fleet

luffing into harbor before diesel transport
       comes for Victorian-mannered boatswain's
            granddaughters. Blue Ridge becoming bluer.

First cadence to envelope Jason in his dragon's-tooth-
       zippered jacket, Mary, our school bus siren
            whose epileptic brain seizes thousands

of times per minute, whose limbs fire as if stung,
       exempt from rules for seen-but-not-heard children.
            Her ecstatic laughter climaxing

over our goings-out and coming-in, beating windward,
       sailors with calenture imagining the ocean
            a green field we might throw ourselves in,

eyes averted to those cliffs Mother climbed once
       and stranded, our raven-haired maiden perched
            on her seatback calling us to the depths.

Ten Thousand Car Hood Lakes Shimmering After Rain

Upended with eye spots
like dark jack about to surface,

Great diving beetles pocket air
under wing, dive

dandled-mahogany-colored
to lake bottoms, birth water tigers,

repel leagues with grassy paddles.
Milt-sift village mothers

crack mirrors
over sons who preen water,

Icarus' opposites,
gold-mottled models of descent,

Dâyuni'sï Cherokee credited
with exhuming creation's first soil

for those deer, foxes, bear
crowding falcons' air,

their star-specked elytra ajar
with oxygen

swum down from the sun
now moon

over stadium light mirages,
giants lost in the world.

Specimens, Mount 28

Dung Beetle

Egyptians say this
world is a digestive loop:
consumers do best only if
they too filter waste from waste

Horned Scarab

Shiny horned devils'
reflection deflected
Sir Charles Darwin's
clerical studies
with soluble mysteries

Mole Beetle

Hard-nosed underground-
gallery mavens, at some point
your wings welded, dismissing
oft-heralded heavens

Click Beetle

Ventral-muscle
contractors who flex
under pressure, teach us
how to snap the catch,
right ourselves with a
backflip

The Law of Contagion

Before missionaries emended
the world to come by abolishing
honeycomb enemy likenesses,

Malay sorcerers tethered beetles
to sacred spirals, reeled
fugitives home.

But after
a Pennsylvania train accordioned,
killing seven, the engineer knew better

than to speak
without an attorney
about what compelled

the 102-m.p.h. vehicle past capacity.
He can't remember,
although the internet will forever

commemorate the uniformed
midshipman en route
to his parents, beside themselves,

Medgar Evers College's Dean of Students
in his doctoral tam and tassel,
even the young truant

who failed to board that morning,
citing a visitor no more arrived than Godot
or you there

nibbling corn flakes
in the antihero's studio,
gray as a medicine man's lute-stiffened fingers

coated with spiders' ashes,
until others discounted such rituals
as sympathetic magic.

Hymenopus

Walking flower, orchid
mimicker with rose-mottled
forelegs ready to drawbridge
on the hapless. Nectar decoy
proffering an empty banquet
before ticklish curtains,
your pollen-lined thorax
a bestial trick of the great
pretender. Perched on a lady
slipper's lip, a bluebottle
buzzes unblinking lavender
ovules, raindrops wetting
the bittersweet chasm
of your badness.

Newly Apparent Sister

Laymen might overlook
entomologists' decade mistaking

Euglossa dilemma for another
solitary orchid bee species, but

the team who discovered
her singularity

hold themselves to higher
standards.

We whose proboscises
discern meatloaf

but fail to distinguish
Joanna's signature body wash

from Indi's gardenia
would not expect

them to parse tibia perfumes
without genetic sequencing,

but daughters
through whom we intuit

bees' needs to individuate
minutest unusual

flowers might
ask that attention.

Sharpshooters

Wanted in Michigan
for being unwanted
on rhododendrons,
leafhoppers hang
from Dorset to London.
Striking blue profiles warn
they'd be better off elsewhere,
though welcome shores
have shrunk like Shrinky
Dinks® 1980s children
baked into hard little plates
they just looked at,
not quite willing or
unwilling to save them.

Cimex Cerebrum

After Damien Laudier (2012)

A bed bug brain wouldn't seem like much
to look at, considering there's precious little

to admire about a blood-fed parasite
westerners eradicated, until the dickens givers

made a comeback as frequent fliers
stowed in shipped furniture,

which was smart enough to warrant
for one photomicrographer slides

of the mechanism that wills its ongoing
detested existence. Vivisection of an origin

no good comes from, except any inherent
in being driven

to live. But under 1000x magnification,
samples bring into focus a reclining colossus,

gaze toward the firmament, face uplifted
as if to catch snowflake-like organelles,

clouds stacked above a brightfield
beyond ideas of right-doing and wrong-doing.

Puddling

American viceroys, admirals
aggregate

in sweated-in places, vie
for squalid-ditch position,

drag indigo robes through royal mud
puddles, leach secretions

from flush barnyards, dabble
goldenrod urine so future tortoiseshell

abdomens will bead julep,
outstretched on dung hammocks

backstroked by ants, guiltless
until, spotted, Corinthian coteries

scatter like cups at a party,
confetti

flitting across kittenish
faces deliquescing sun lint.

Bloody-nosed Beetle, Stopped in His Heathland Trek, Explains Intimacy to a Welsh Boy Who Thinks He Found A Pet

I will never be your dog, boy,
nor my spit a trick you can master,
nor come loping dumb
across goose grass
to lick sweat or tears
from silt-soft flesh.

Won't scratch a post
with dew-beaded tarsi,
bat a tuft of crochet mouse,
swim to your finger,
nibble an extended biscuit,
make puppy eyes at you

across hedgerows
with ultraviolet lenses
you don't know to envy.
Defenses spring eternal—
claws, clicks, self-burial.
See my carmine drop

about to drip
you who run to middle-school bathrooms
hands fluttering like killdeer
away from the nest,
your smirch-begging Oxford
so ready to disappoint mother,

I know you.
Look how a miniature pointillist portrait
spatters your cupped hand,
the expression on your face
of curious terror that would cast me
far from you.

Of Course

After Louis C.K.

Of course Jains are quaint with their little
brooms clearing paths of smaller beings,
but think of all the bugs I've crushed
as grounds for retribution. Please.
I've got to catch the train, shortcut
the park with deli sushi for my points-scoring
lunch date picnic. But *maybe,*
maybe the nobodies who take time
for innumerable, thankless others are compensated
somehow—not in that great beyond, but real-time
sifted puffs purling free of thrips and gnats,
sipped under white cloths
masking blissful smiles.

H.D.'s Bees

Sad

Blighted chestnuts fall, fruit-
rich seeds cracked to slip inside
caked earth, little death-throe lock snapped,
switch thrown and plummet on
until touched. Minions of sweetness
patrol mophead hydrangeas whose
aging lacecaps green. Over. Over.
Over. Over. The flayed Générale
Vicomtesse de Vibraye blossoms dry,
papery, violet on the plant.

Sorrowful

Hanyuan County pear farmers inseminate
flowers with paint brushes, dunk
ineradicable lice in barrel-bath insecticide.
Between grass blades, a carpet of corpses
muffle white petals, shudder
the way discarded whale corpses
bloated, bobbed on the ocean, then sank,
ambergris gotten
to dot a neck, blubber melted into lamps.

Withdrawn

Lovers safe deposit sulk, punish
what every sweet-seeker knows to ingest. Bitterness
chews out and wads thick,
golden strands pulled from another mouth.
Dance second shift to the bluebell patch,
lean so far the tether almost snaps
with a thrust before the long trip back.

Loss

The shepherd long undreamt
wanders hive mind's starry fields, sows
a new pastoral inside Mars-One-Way applicants.
The ship has Joellen's name on it,
her boyfriend says. No bouquets to send back
from the planet whose opiate heat warp grips
her heart. Who could compete?
But planet nostalgia, he might count on that
peal of firsts—the sheep's bleat gated between thighs
to be sheared that teaches its tender how to love.

The Cove

Last night, in-laws barreled over the same
hayfield my folks and I plodded
on foot to collect downed limbs,

their pickup truck tailing a footloose
herd, rutting flooded grass stems, ruining
cattle lunches.

Good fences wash out.
Storm-uprooted water racks
create archways cattle walk through,

princes of damnable-mannered kingdoms
in which hairline-hitching ticks preceded
fawns and children, as if the bitty leaches

wanted their red cells' sucker-asking juiciness
into being, love them
the way thistles nuzzle ornamental grasses.

IV.

When we who knew you by name
are gone, what will they call you?

—Wendell Berry

Insect Time

Consult a termite queen
before she scratches off
her nuptial flight wings
and after, when she sweats fat
inside her earthen capsule
where she once nestled with her king,
nymphs in love with solitude.
Who counts seconds when every third
she lays another quarter billionth
egg. She grows translucent.
Colony-whirr fills the cathedral
above her, an insistent dispenser
whose stillness releases everything
that is not it in static white
procession, like bubbles
drawn around captioned thought.

Old Glassy Speaks Her Peace

What you call Dame de Paris,
water peacock, silver pin,
dragonflies don't bother with,
name neither ourselves nor each
long-legged crane fly, piss ant.
Over 300 million years, aloe strops
drop into mangroves, wingspans
wide as crows borne aloft on oxygen
fields imprint in what will be rock.
You move on.
Find pure water, attend a body
call it caddis, mosquito, mayfly,
we've caught it, flat abdomens ready
for sex in the air, life in the air.
Night spills shot down marble halls
of cicadas. We barely hear it,
smell no croissants, diesel burp.
We are diamond-minded
hunters. Little nuns, you say!
eyes in back of our heads
like the devil's grandmother.
We are older than the devil,
youngsters, older than sand spun
into glass to which you compare us.
Older than your oldest word,
our diaphanous oars shear light
from air, 30,000 lenses scanning
your baubles with indifference.

Heaven of Delight

(2002) Jan Fabre

One million six hundred
jewel beetle elytra
plate the Brussels
Royal Palace ceiling,
an emerald Aegean
eddying in from one
hundred sundry tributaries.
The chandelier a virid,
brigandine teat attendees
suckle, wingless
occipital cortexes lifted.

Scientists Film Inside A Flying Insect

"If we can reproduce it..."
—*BBC News*

An x-rayed blowfly
in action wheels inside, buckles,

a mid-stride Derby horse
pleasuring itself

against air. Slowed
for human eyes,

miniscule muscles
curl the whole rower

the way a neck
rocks a girl on the swings,

her arches pushed
to the sky.

The pull
of life

recognizable
now by fried

mother boards, one
hundred little deaths

attempting to lift
a tiny electric

aeronaut, buzzing,
from the earth.

Comma

Ovum, a threaded star
hanging in limbo, wax-lined chorion
from which capsule emerges a dog-toothed
Christmas ornament, inflated
with hemolymph, vulnerable
to predators until its wet wings, not yet ready
for takeoff, air dry.

Specimens, Mount 48

Owlfly

Haides' orchard
steward emerges
at twilight, hawks cabbage
moths and aphids,
shushing screeches midair

Euphaea

Red-listed damsel,
your wings part a shadow
overhead, blue as a robin's egg,
warm as the highest scarlet
terror warning

Chrysina

Tinsel on cedars,
Salvadoran beetles shine from
receding forest margins, in hope,
pathetic as lovers we never knew
loved us, of candle-lit rescue

Nanosella

World's Smallest Beetle
title contender nestles in
spore tunes, taking pulls
from pipe organs, meek
inheritors of the feast to come

The Snout Beetles' Epistle

We cat-face your tomatoes, gardeners,
crescent-slit fruit skin, deposit eggs in pulp
flesh. You fear

those peachy cheeks too will pucker,
upset symmetry, but we make better
stone fruits, which make better beetles.

There's no such thing as even, Steven.

Crisp apples crush larvae unless
humped backs quadruple thickness
to bore scarred tissue.

Sour-faced plums gob market baskets
but set off unblemished shoulders.
Pearls shine equally from pigs' necks.

Zebra Crickets

Black-and-white-
striped crickets prick flesh-
toned bipeds' costume needs,
break Jack White into Denial
Twist riffs, but that flamboyant
skeleton won't shame us,
gorgeous. We'll throw down
our bones to buy couture jackets
that outmode the railroad,
Breton, candy, and kitten
stripe in one fell post-Bengal
swoop of 3D print.

Fanny Howe's Bees

Tremulous

Static sweeps a lone brizz past,
a buzz without a we, a zilch.
Before 1050, a *beh,* a *bitte,* a *bij,* a *bini*
fainter by the minute, a Sunkist®-fuzzed
honey hex that can't be passed. Not this summer
will we scale back, when we just got
that poolside cup with its slick lip
of caramel sweat.

Murky

Dark tick of ice cap melt
butters red clay into river mud,
trash bags stuffed with plastic-
collared squid. The meme dots
six-pack wrap we cut and crush
peppers to our chests spritzed
with systemic neonics—
words we don't know to distrust.

Dread

A meeting room dynamic shifts
before a woman eyeballing not a bee but
an insect evolved to stop pests, and herself,
EpiPen®-less. What we can see to correct
we face uncertain whose place it is to act. We sit with
the wasp, motionless, track its whereabouts,
a family flagging Mother on the Internet
back from deployment, holding her own in an Ironman,
them no readier than last time for her absence.

Estranged

A beekeeper hums to keep
companionable grit in back of the throat,
a wine-wet wheat berry
chewed soft. The sky gone,
we went to the Superdome
after the flood, like an arc.

Acres Green©

On film, synthetic Beamer Bees
        designed to pollinate technotopia
                streak fields in soft neon waves.

The Power of 8 Team illustrates alternatives
        for living without honey
                bees with a jar of pink syrup,

studies natural footage to recreate
        a firefly swarm in LED fiber optics,
                programs Beamers to return

to the hive with a bugle modem
        that sounds below human hearing—for all appearances,
                the way they are called back now.

Of the Feet of Flies

After Robert Hooke (1665)

Two pinnate talons
per microscopic fly palm
esteem otherwise common
fauna, your Highness.
Note its ability to clasp
claws like index finger
to thumb and hang
from even a pore of glass
its chandelier body.
A dangling pendant
would be the envy
of single-digit fleas
and mites, were they,
like us, prone to covet
defter neighbors, but
beyond comparison,
God's vision numbers
your Majesty's argent hairs
and ephemerids' triple ankle
joints filigreed to glissade
lightly over the most
fragrant earth.

Long-tongued Flower Sipper

Fallen tree bark
blended into forest floor

detritus, rubbed-rabbit's-pelt umber,
freckled-hawk mauve, ash

thrown over your forewings
like a lucky salt pinch.

Curls of blonde sand ravel
cycloramas, flying off.

Grant us this wish,
seam rippers—lend us a poplar

billow for our hindwings,
if we had wings

to snap the backdrop, exiting,
death's head tattooed on our napes.

Carrion Sylph

Burying beetles strip
ribs matte, fur cloak doe
leftovers, floss death-
opened jaws, no fatter
for all that ridded slick.
Out of a glossless socket
pops a parson urchin
mites hitch to the next
defenseless task. Charon's
air ferry over Lethe,
wings flaring a cornflower-
blue butterfly mimic
they can only see
who are left.

The Long Timer

No endurance run
outpaces leafcutter ants'

month-long,
four-minute-mile

marathons or
outnumbers pupae

laved and licked
before another virgin queen

emerges and workers
die ignobly,

second only
to human deforesters

burning Amazon-basin
tracts like cherry-Victorian

loveseats for tinder. Except
these preppers carpet

gardens in biohazard-swabbing
fungi, knit

filamentous frost
under which spit-

oiled strike wheels
clock distant wins.

Yam Weevil

Infinitely susceptible
to downtrodden
or gobble, weevil
designers are constantly
upping the panoply
of options, like this outfit
in a blue-banded tunic
with tropical longitudinal
pinstripes, perfect for
afternoon executive meetings
or working lunches
in five-star restaurants
where presentation is so
crucial waiters will garnish
the cush cush if a chef hasn't.
Cerulean and sea green
bedeck each hind wing
and antenna, but toe tips
are the real touch, edged
with a downy-haired
yellow aura so that even left
entourage-less, he is
not without limelight.

Amy Wright is the Nonfiction Editor of Zone
3 Press, Coordinator of Creative Writing at
Austin Peay State University, and the author of
five chapbooks. *Everything in the Universe* is her
first full-length poetry collection. Her writing
appears in a number of journals including
Kenyon Review, Southern Poetry Anthology
(Volumes III and VI), and *Tupelo Quarterly.*
She has been awarded with two Peter Taylor
Fellowships for the *Kenyon Review* Writers'
Workshop, an Individual Artist's Fellowship
from the Tennessee Arts Commission, and
a fellowship to the VCCA. She and William
Wright co-authored *Creeks of the Upper South.*
Her second poetry collection, *Cracker Sonnets,*
is forthcoming. For more information, visit
www.awrightawright.com.

CPSIA information can be obtained
at www.ICGtesting.com
Printed in the USA
LVOW11s2324270417
532507LV00001B/77/P

9 781604 542370